T0087012

Sing in a Season

Bob Chilcott

for SATB and piano or small ensemble

vocal score

OXFORD
UNIVERSITY PRESS

OXFORD
UNIVERSITY PRESS

Great Clarendon Street, Oxford OX2 6DP,
United Kingdom

Oxford University Press is a department of the University of Oxford.
It furthers the University's objective of excellence in research, scholarship,
and education by publishing worldwide. Oxford is a registered trade mark of
Oxford University Press in the UK and in certain other countries

© Oxford University Press 2023

Bob Chilcott has asserted his right under the Copyright, Designs
and Patents Act, 1988, to be identified as the Composer of this Work

All rights reserved. No part of this publication may be reproduced,
stored in a retrieval system, or transmitted, in any form or by any means,
without the prior permission in writing of Oxford University Press

Permission to perform this work in public (except in the course of divine worship)
should normally be obtained from a local performing right licensing organization,
unless the owner or the occupier of the premises being used already holds
a licence from such an organization. Likewise, permission to make and
exploit a recording of these works should be obtained from a
local mechanical copyright licensing organization

Enquiries concerning reproduction outside the scope of the above
should be directed to the Music Rights Department, Oxford University Press,
at music.permissions.uk@oup.com or at the address above

ISBN 978–0–19–356304–9

Music and text origination by Katie Johnston
Printed in Great Britain on acid-free paper by
Halstan & Co. Ltd, Amersham, Bucks.

Contents

1. Follow the music 5
2. A Gift so in Tune 22
3. Sing in a Season 35

Composer's note

Sing in a Season was written for the 50th anniversary of the Plano Civic Chorus, which began in the autumn of 2022. The request for this piece came from their conductor, Ralph Stannard, in early 2021, when we were slowly beginning to emerge from the Covid pandemic. Under the circumstances, we felt we needed a piece that could express what music, and particularly singing, which we had all missed so much, might mean to us. The poet Charles Bennett, in his three elegant and ultimately transformative poems, urges us to look to the diversity and richness of the surrounding natural world for ways to find our voice. The work concludes with an inspirational call from Charles's pen with the words: 'So may our lives, improvised as we go along, now and then take flight to become a song'.

Duration: *c.*15 minutes

An alternative accompaniment for small ensemble (fl, ob, cl in A, hn in F, timp, org) is available for purchase (ISBN 978–0–19–356581–4)

Commissioned for the 50th anniversary of the Plano Civic Chorus; Ralph F. Stannard, Artistic Director

Sing in a Season

1. Follow the music

Charles Bennett (b. 1954)

BOB CHILCOTT

Music © Oxford University Press 2023. Text © Charles Bennett. Reproduced by permission of the author.

Printed in Great Britain

OXFORD UNIVERSITY PRESS, MUSIC DEPARTMENT, GREAT CLARENDON STREET, OXFORD OX2 6DP

The Moral Rights of the Composer have been asserted. Photocopying this copyright material is ILLEGAL.

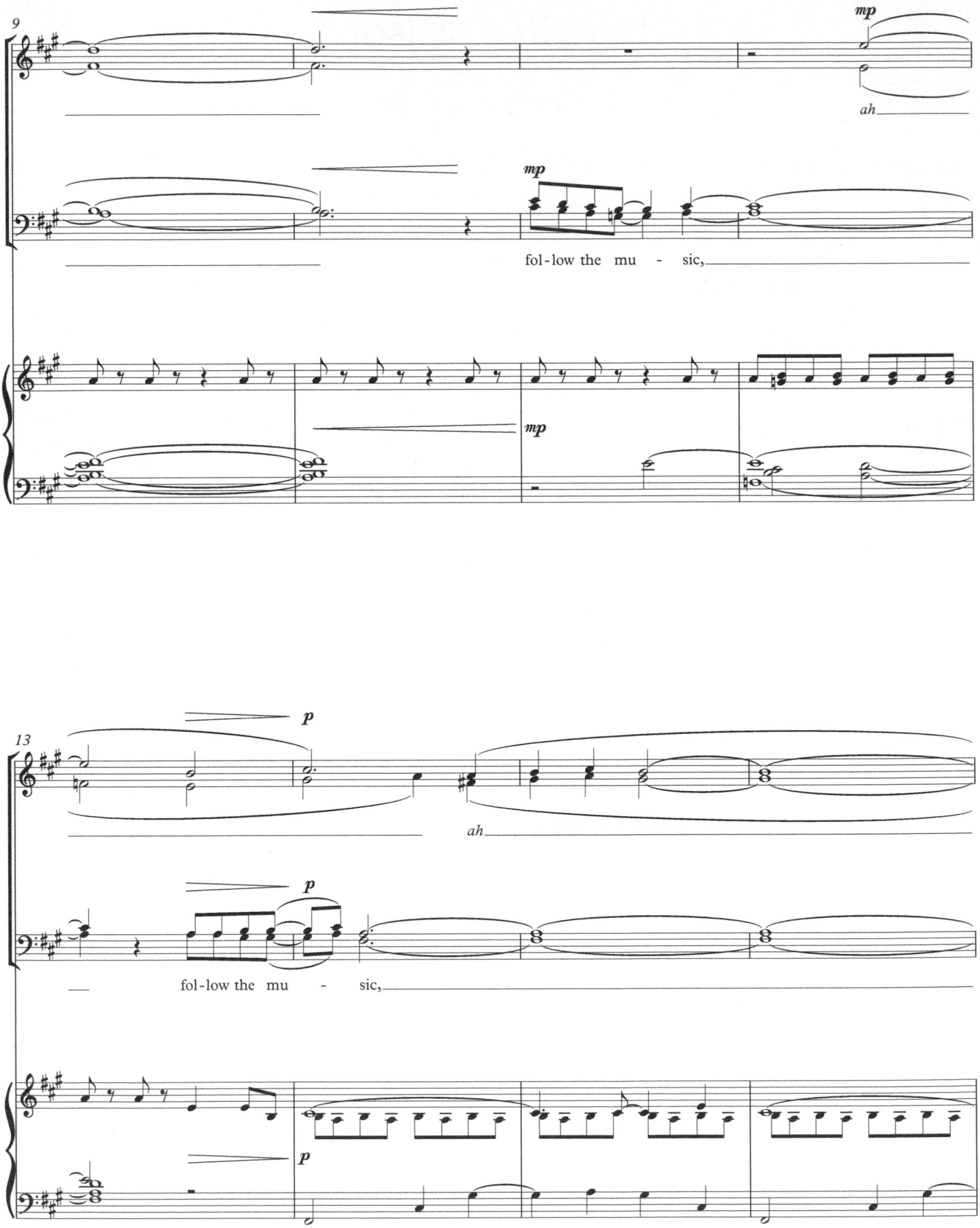
9
mp
ah
mp
fol-low the mu - sic,
mp
13
p
ah
p
fol-low the mu - sic,
p

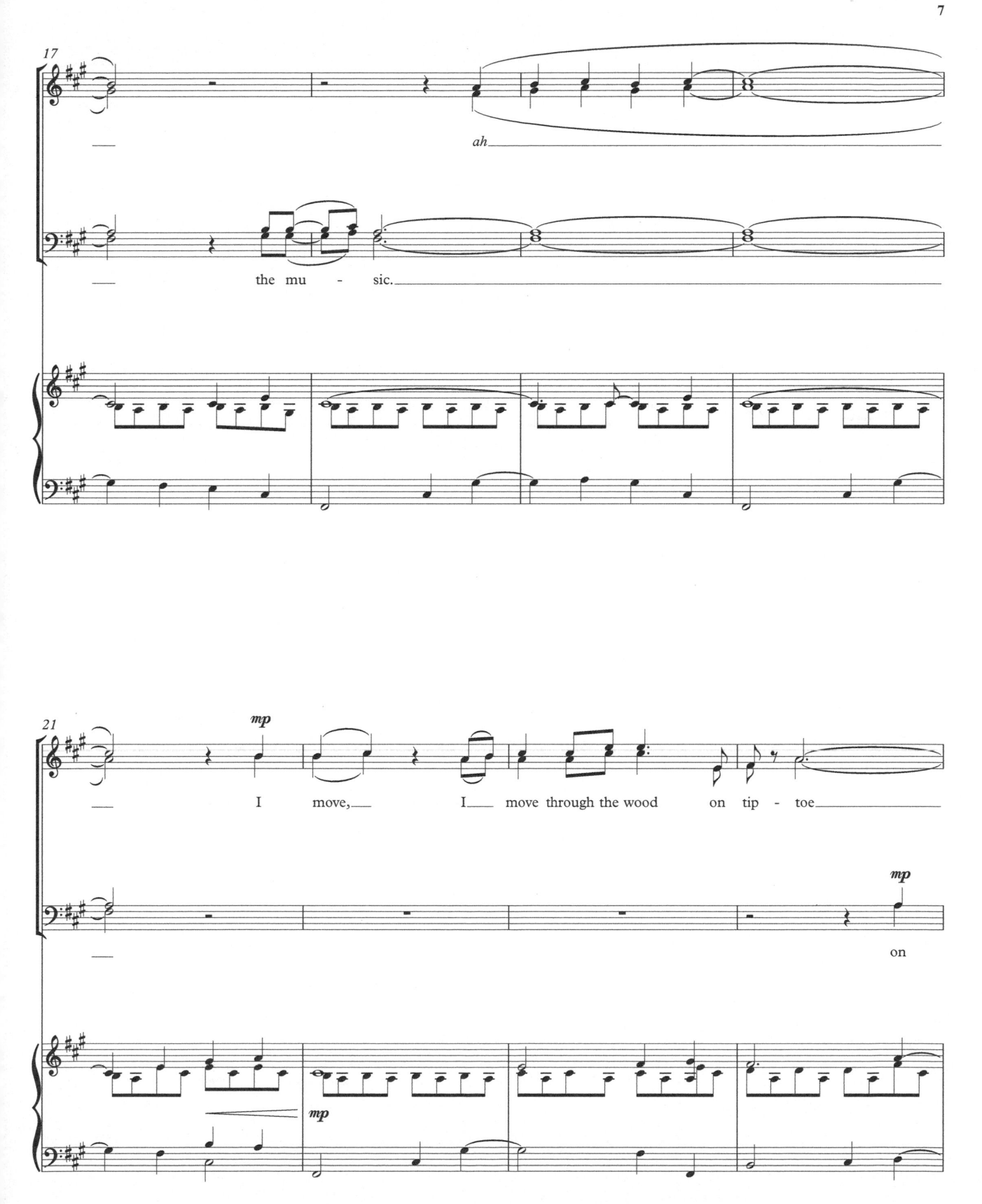
17
ah
the mu - sic.
21
mp
I move, I move through the wood on tip - toe
mp
on
mp

25
from one song, from one song to the next.
tip - toe, tip - toe, to the
29
mf
bright trail, a bright
Their mu - sic is a bright trail, bright
next.
mf
mf

33
f
trail, a net - work of ae - rial path -
f
f
37
- ways.
p

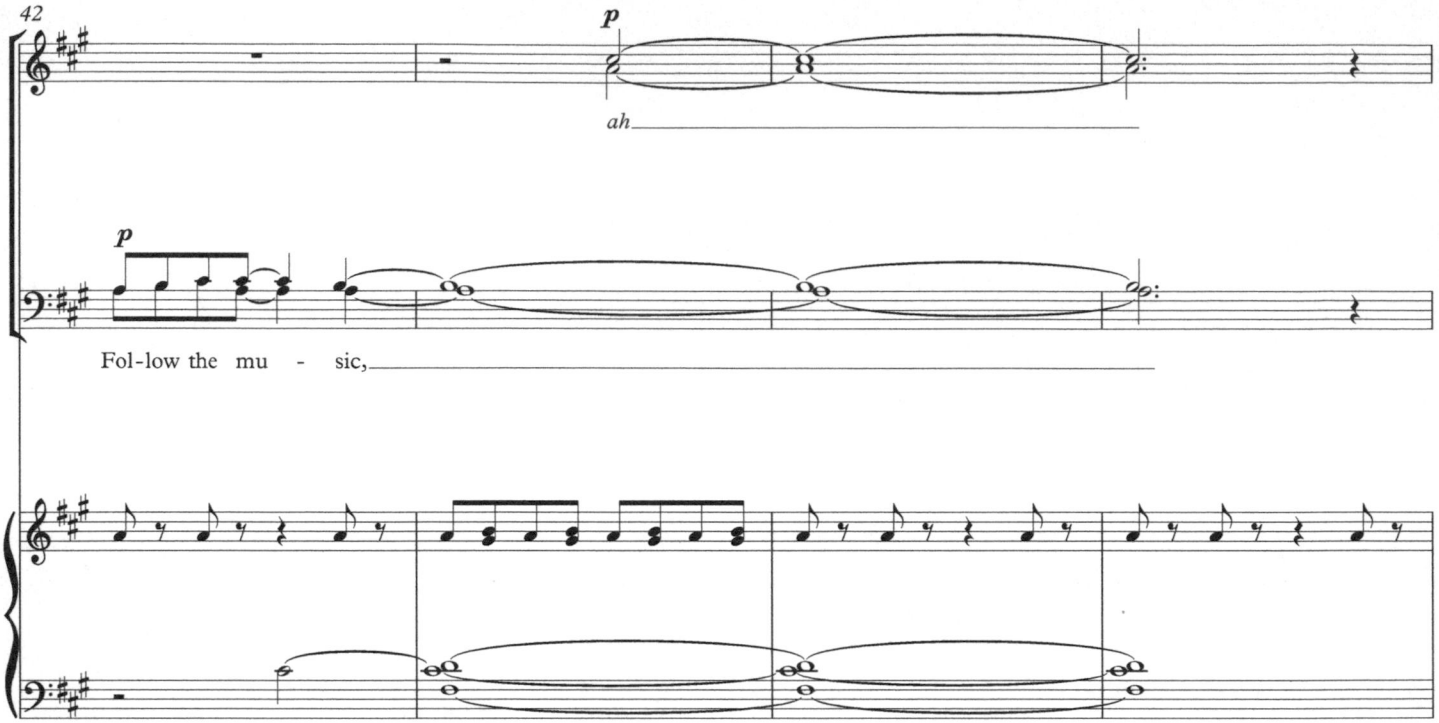
42
p
ah
p
Fol-low the mu - sic,

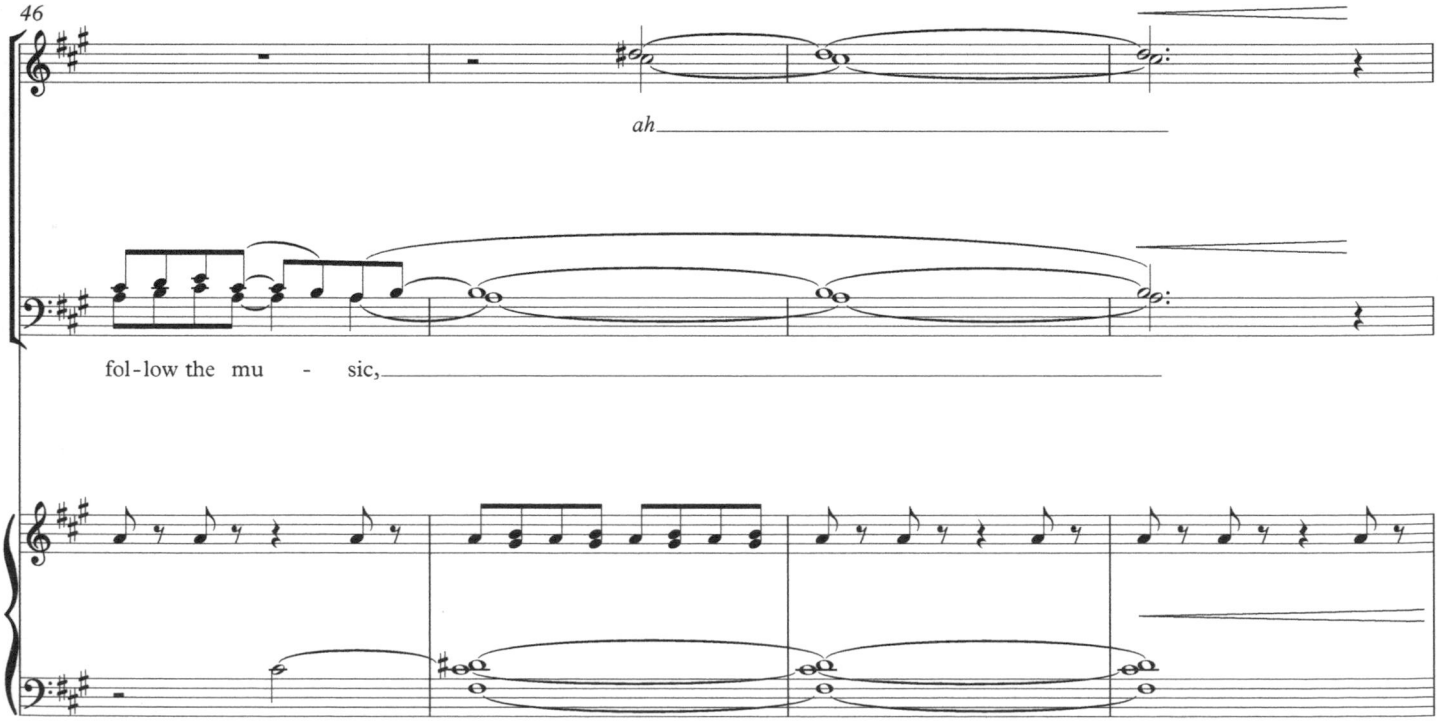
46
ah
fol-low the mu - sic,

50
mp
p
ah
ah
mp
p
fol-low the mu - sic,
fol-low the mu - sic,
mp
p

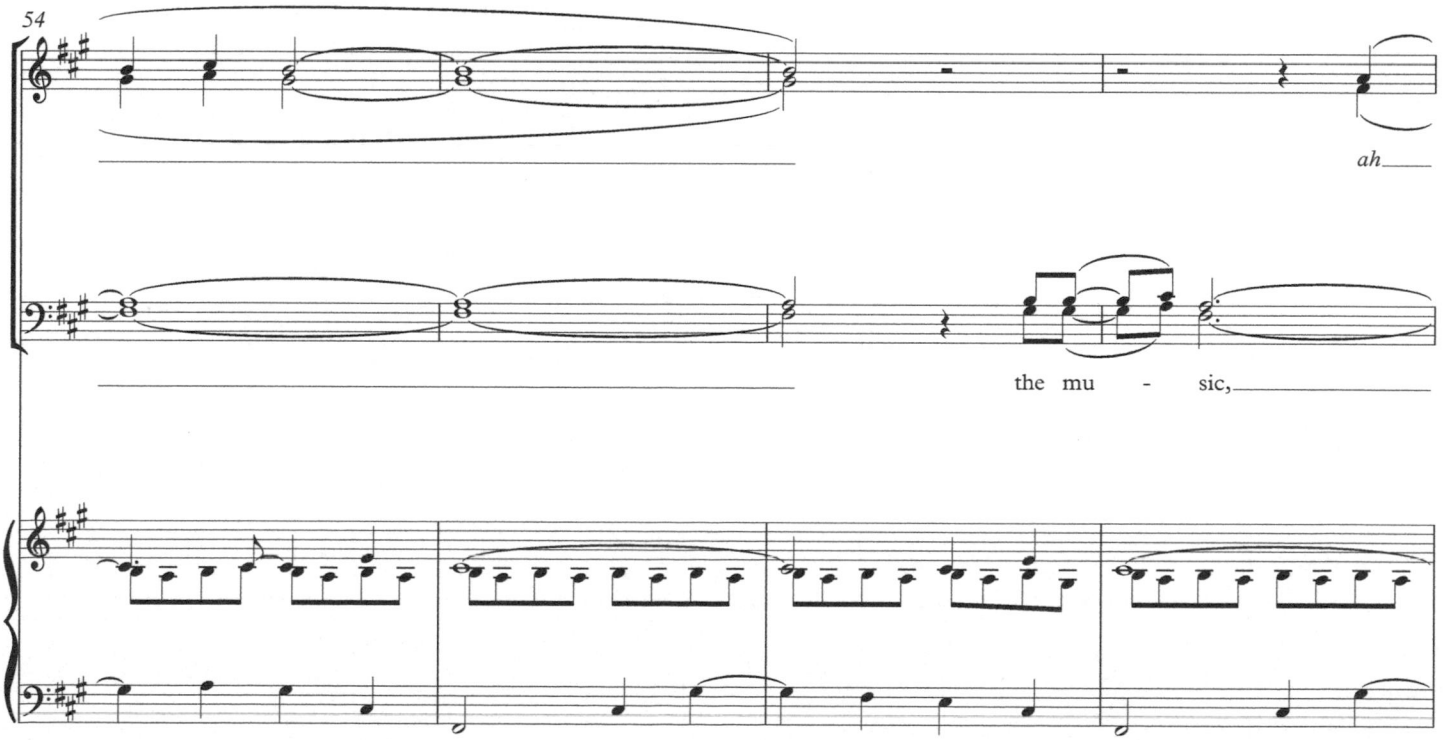
54
ah
the mu - sic,

58
mp
ah
T. & B. unis.
mp
Down to the
mp
62
mf
ah
ah
foot - prints,
mf
T.
B.
stream where the deer have left their foot - prints, their foot - prints, their
mf

66
past blue - bells and
espress.
past blue - bells and
foot - prints,
espress.
71
yel - low arch - an - gel,
yel - low arch - an - gel, o - ver the trunk of a

75
S.
fresh - ly fall - en birch.
A.
mp
fresh - ly fall - en birch, fall - en
T.
mp
fresh - ly fall - en birch, fall - en
B.
fresh - ly fall - en birch.
79
p
ah
p
birch.
ah
p
birch.
p

83
ah
ah
ah
ah
87

91
mp cresc.
I walk with - out know - ing where I am,
mp cresc.
I walk with - out know - ing where I
mp cresc.
I walk with - out know - ing where I
mp cresc.
I walk, walk with - out know - ing where I
mp cresc.
RH
LH
95
f
luck - y to be lost in the woods with
am, luck - y to be lost in the
am, luck - y to be lost in the
am, luck - y to be lost in the

99
no - thing bet - ter to do,
f
woods with no - thing bet - ter to
f
woods with no - thing bet - ter to
f
woods with no - thing bet - ter to
f
102
to do than
do, to do, to do than
do, to do, to do than
do, to do, than

106
mf
fol - low the mu - sic, fol - low the mu - sic,
mf
fol - low the mu - sic, fol - low the mu - sic,
mf
fol - low the mu - sic, fol - low the mu - sic,
mf
fol - low the mu - sic, fol - low the mu - sic,
mf
110
f
fol - low the mu - sic, fol - low the mu - sic,
f
fol - low the mu - sic, fol - low the mu - sic,
f
fol - low the mu - sic, fol - low the mu - sic,
f
fol - low the mu - sic, fol - low the mu - sic,
f

114
ff
f
fol - low the mu - sic,
fol - low the mu - sic, fol - low the mu - sic,
fol - low the mu - sic, fol - low the mu - sic,
fol - low the mu - sic, mu - sic,
118
mf dim.
un - til I
mu - - sic, un - til I
mu - - sic, un - til I
un - til I

122
p
find my way.
p
find my way.
p
find my way.
p
find my way.
p
126
ah
ah

130
pp
ah
pp
ah
pp
134
ah
ah

2. A Gift so in Tune

9
mp
p
- clined, de - clined, Grey seals Sour - ly
mp
p
mp
p
13
mp
mf
f
chimed, sour - ly
sour - ly chimed,
chimed, chimed, sour - ly chimed,
sour - ly, sour - ly chimed,
mp
mf
f
chimed,
mp
mf
f

17
chimed, sour - ly chimed.
mf
mp
chimed, sour - ly chimed, sour - ly
mf
mp
mf
mp
20
f
chimed.
They wailed and howled As night fell
f
p
sub. f

24
grey, green notes
mf
slow - ly, grey, grey, green notes So me - lan -
me - lan -
mf
mf
28
mp
p
-cho - ly, me - lan - cho - ly, me - lan - cho - ly.
mp
p
-cho - ly, me - lan - cho - ly,
mp
p

32
A little faster ♩ = c.63
S.
mp espress.
What_
A.
mp espress.
What_
A little faster ♩ = c.63
mp
36
shall_ I_ make_ Of a gift so in tune With the north - ern_ star_ And a
shall_ I_ make_ Of a gift so in tune With the north - ern_ star_ And a

39
mf
mp
bro - ken, bro - ken moon? A bro - ken moon.
mf
mp
bro - ken, bro - ken moon? A bro - ken moon.
mf
mp
43
T.
mp cresc.
What
B.
mp cresc.
What

46
S.
mp
A gift so in tune,
A.
mp cresc.
A gift so in tune, And a
T.
shall I make Of a gift so in tune With the north - ern star And a
B.
shall I make Of a gift so in tune With the north - ern star And a
cresc.
49
f
And a bro - ken moon? A bro - ken
bro - ken, bro - ken moon? A bro - ken moon.
bro - ken, bro - ken moon, bro - ken moon?
bro - ken, bro - ken moon, bro - ken moon?

52
mp
poco rit.
moon.
poco rit.
mp
56
a tempo
p
Then I heard them say: Lis - ten and
p
Then I heard them say: Lis - ten and
p
Then I heard them say: Lis - ten and
p
Then I heard them say: Lis - ten and
a tempo
p

60
learn, lis - ten and learn, At its low - est
cresc.
learn, lis - ten and learn, At its low - est
cresc.
learn, lis - ten and learn, At its low - est
cresc.
learn, lis - ten and learn, At its low - est
cresc.
cresc.
63
ebb The tide will turn, the tide will turn, will
ebb The tide will turn, the tide will turn, will
ebb The tide will turn, the tide will turn, will
ebb The tide will turn, the tide will turn, will

poco rit.
a tempo
66
f
ff
turn, will turn. The
turn, the tide will turn, will turn.
turn, the tide will turn, will turn. The
turn, the tide will turn, will turn. The
poco rit.
a tempo
70
fu - ture said: See what I'm bring - ing, Some sor - row, sor - row, yes, But
The fu - ture said: See what I'm bring - ing, Some sor - row, yes, But
fu - ture said: See what I'm bring - ing, Some sor - row, yes, But
fu - ture said: See what I'm bring - ing, Some sor - row, sor - row,

73
f
al - so sing - ing, al - so sing - ing,
al - so sing - ing, sing - ing, sing - ing,
al - so, al - so sing - ing, al - so sing - ing,
yes, But al - so sing - ing, sing -
poco rit.
a tempo
76
mf dim.
sing - ing.
- ing.
p

80
poco rit.
poco rit.
mp
84
a tempo
p
Some sor - row, yes,
p
Some sor - row, yes, some sor - row,
p
Some sor - row, yes, some sor - row,
p
Some sor - row, yes, some sor - row,
a tempo
p

88
rit.
But al - so sing - ing, sing - ing, sing - ing,
yes, But al - so sing - ing, sing - ing, sing - ing,
yes, But al - so sing - ing, sing - ing, sing - ing,
yes, But al - so sing - ing, sing - ing, sing - ing,
rit.
92
pp
sing - ing, sing - - ing.
sing - ing, sing - - ing.
sing - ing, sing - - ing.
sing - ing, sing - - ing.
pp

3. Sing in a Season

10
S.
wind,
S.
A.
f
a cold sky
T.
B.
f
Blown from their roost in - to a cold sky a - bove the
13
a - bove the elm, in - to a cold sky, they laughed and
elm, in - to a cold sky, they laughed and danced, they

16
danced, danced, on the wind, the wind,
laughed and danced on the wind, on the wind,
19
mf
and the shape they cre-
mf
ff dim.
mf

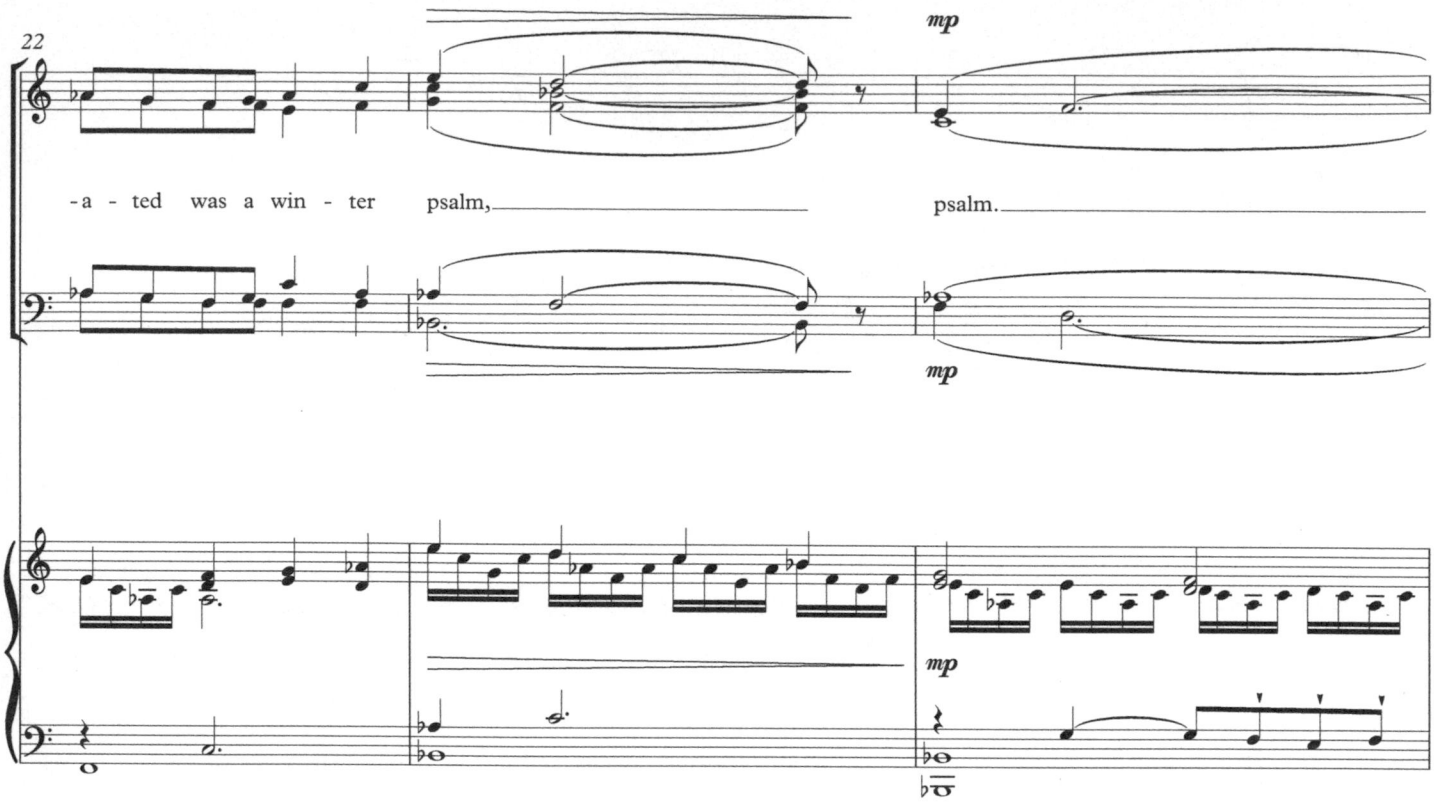
22
mp
-a - ted was a win - ter psalm,
psalm.
mp
mp

25
p
And then I knew, and
p
p

28
mp
this out - of - tune ca - co - pho - ny was
then I knew,
mp
ah
mp
31
mf
how the rooks and jack - daws sang,
and
f
mf
ah
ah
mf

34
made, from those dark, dark notes,
dis -
f
and made, made from those dark notes,
f
37
mf dim.
- joint - ed har - - mo - ny,
mf dim.
mf dim.

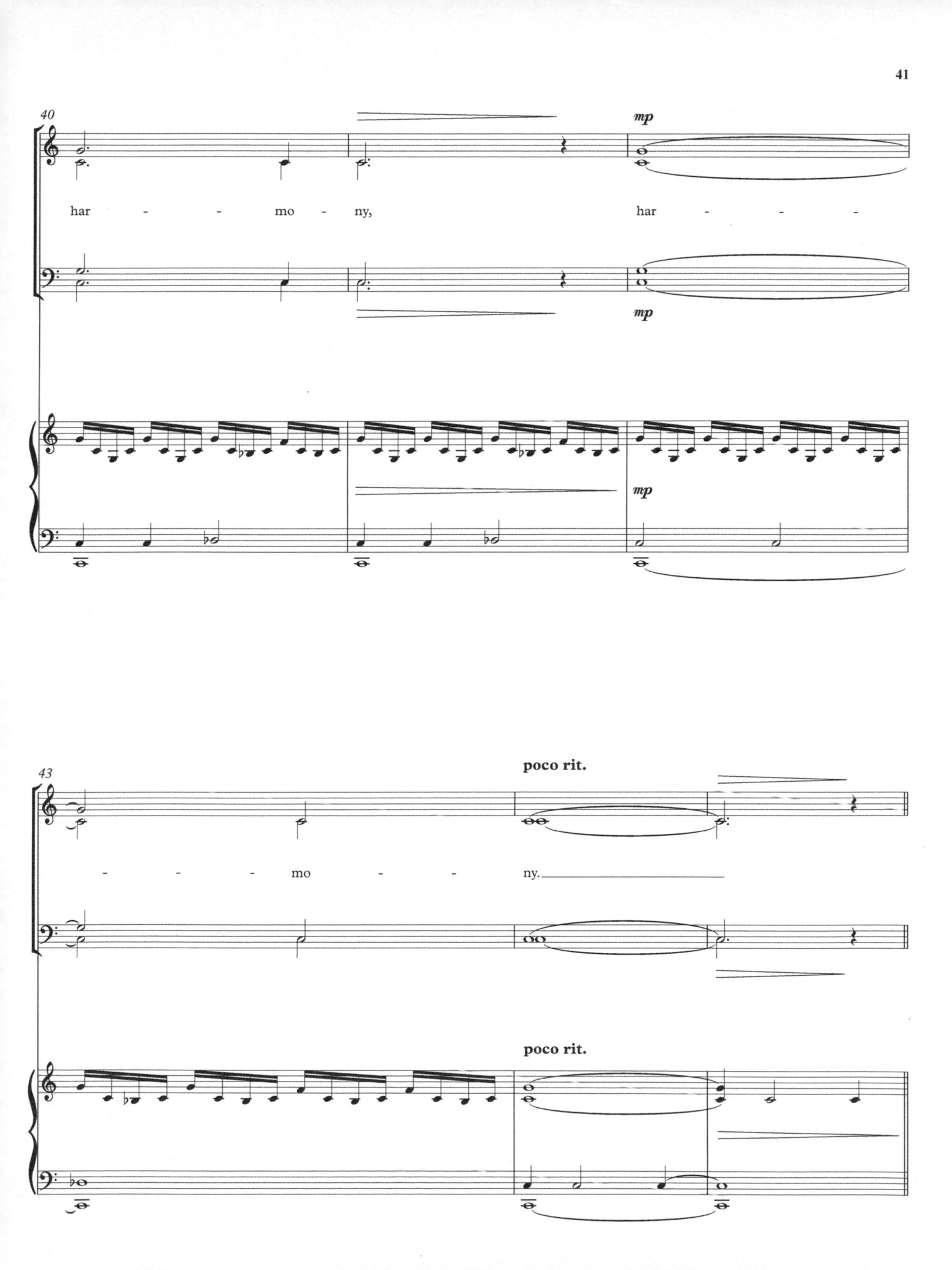
40
mp
har - - mo - ny, har - - -
mp
mp
43
poco rit.
- - - mo - - ny.
poco rit.

46
A little slower ♩ = c.84
S.
A.
p
It made me think: if rag - ged
p
49
mp
mf
birds can re - joice and sing in a sea - son such as this, I
mp
mf
52
S.
A.
ought to spread my wings and find my voice.
T.
B.
mf
It

55
ah
ah
made me think: if rag - ged birds can re - joice and sing in a sea - son
58
f
I ought to spread my wings and find my
such as this,
f
f

poco accel.
61
my voice, my voice, my
voice, my voice, my voice, and find my
poco accel.
Tempo I
65
ff
voice.
ff
SOPRANOS
f risoluto
So may our lives,
Tempo I
ff
f

68
S.
so may our lives, im - pro-vised as we go a - long,
71
now and then, now and then take flight, take
74
S.
flight.
S.
A.
f risoluto
So may our lives, so may our
T.
B.
f risoluto
So may our lives, so may our lives,

77
lives, our lives,
lives,
as we go a - long,
im - pro - vised
79
now and then take flight, now and then take

82
flight, now and then take flight to be - come a
rit.
ff
85
song, a song, a song.
ff
rit.
ff
ff